THE KING OF RIMES

the claim of the throne

Ziad Dib Jreige

Also by Ziad Dib Jreige

The Nightingale: His poems and paintings of dawn

THE KING OF RIMES

the claim of the throne

Ziad Dib Jreige

Inkfeathers Publishing
www.inkfeathers.com

The King of Rimes
Written by Ziad Dib Jreige
Paperback Edition

First Published in India in 2022
by Inkfeathers Publishing, New Delhi 110095

ISBN 9789390882748

www.inkfeathers.com

The King of Rimes

Upon the throne, where few had shone,
There I shall sit, and never quit,
Whether of stone, or feelings flown,
My words with wit, your hearts will hit.
In days so bright, or deep black night,
You'll find my lines, as old fine wines,
Pesky but right, with royal might,
Like soaring pines and climbing vines.
Some may say, with clear dismay,
That I'm bighead, but I'm instead,
Starting today, what you all may,
Like and spread, as endless thread.
Write and share, do not just stare,
Your words are too gorgeous and true,
But if you dare, approach my chair,
Good luck though, I'll bewitch you.

A Quote

A love for a rose, can be lost in its thorns

Naivety

I sat under a blue sky
And wished for a cloud
I closed my weary eye
And oh! A wind loud
Blew on my warm face
I opened my sight
And clouds were in race
Closing up all light
I then wished for rain
And a rain did fall
Then I wanted sun again
But vain was my call

Sonnet 01

Not one memory of a cradle's song
Nor a melody in the ranging ears,
Not even a distant echo along
The curvy tunnel of the racing years.
Not an image in head of the first sight
Nor a vision about the colours seen,
Not even a notion if it was night
Or a cloudy shot, or a sunlit scene.
Not an idea about what might look
After the trip out of this very land,
Maybe a thought coming from a book
Maybe a rib, in the troubled sea sand.
Behold now, a love is widening the sky
Pleasuring the mind, the ear and the eye.

A Foe (Haiku)

I nurtured my self,
So well, until it became,
My worst obstacle.

A Quote

Hesitation is the tomb of creativity.

A Feast (Haiku)

Before the night leaves,
A tiger's eating the deer
That ate the oak leaves.

Sonnet 2

One moment it takes to pour light around
As if a painting is getting replaced
An explosion free of any sound
As if darkness is by sunrays outpaced
A drastic change, so marvellous, so fast
Appearing slow, and messing with time
As if a million masks, that all will last
And across the enchanted sky they climb
Upon the horizon a burning spell
Is dancing bright with colourless fire
As if from a deep dark and silent well
Freedom is out, with heavenly attire
Thus, shall all of us witness and see
A mighty dawn, upon mountain and sea.

A Memory

Around the fire where it raged
We sat unable to move
As if the winter, young aged
Had its strength to prove
Oh, that harsh and freezing kiss
That night had left on walls
Now I crave and seek and miss
When memory beats and calls

Dear Pleasure (Haiku)

I drew a thick line
Between my self and pleasure,
My self erased it.

Sonnet 03

A new dawn, the dark reef is now vivid
Busy damsels around the corals race
A shark hungry stalks a grouper timid
But what is befalling that morning pace?
Oh behold! The waves are in decay
As if the sea is now a confined pond
Oh! Behold! The shark has left its prey
Shall no hunter kill and shall no bound
Restrain the eyes from the shiny tail
That impels and draws upon the sand
Big shells of dreams which tell the tale
Of beauty and fear that comes from land
A mesmerising pure face with long hair
In the deep, with a heart full of fresh air

Bright Dark (Haiku)

I dreamt a dream wild
Where dim Winter called bright Spring
My dear unborn child

Sonnet 04

I sought apricity when beneath the sun
Last winter I sat and drank a thick wine
My thoughts wandered and to you did run
I felt cold and warm and tired and fine
I poured in the glass more of the red
As death had poured in you its wave
I could not recall what you did and said
But saw you scream in a burning grave
In vain I tried to reach out and help
With a drop of wine your parching look
Gazing with all the flames that skelped
At me and weeping a burnt love that shook
This winter, when sun breaks the cold rain
Will I drink some wine in its rays again?

A Grave (Haiku)

It's simple, you see,
The very seed you thought dead,
Is now a strong tree.

Unaware

I paid a fortune just to know
Where Happiness could be found
I was told that above the snow
The mountain top it crowned.
From my deep valley I rose
And years to there I spent
Till I reached with bare toes
The summit with big content.
But no, Happiness did glare
Cold, tired, all by my own
Down the valley I gave a stare
My Happiness glowed down there.

Sonnet 05

Have not my breath taken yet, 'ere I'm done,
Around the temple I walk, with no rest
Those who have found a way in, have won
I feel silence approaching my loud chest.
In circles, I stride searching for a door,
Beseeching each and every passing soul
Even the stones of the walls and the floor
I urge, but earless and blind they pass all.
Of what can I think save a place to hide
Away from the wrath of my own deeds,
When my soul is called, and I'm still outside
Then I'll be consumed by my own needs.
All at once, everyone is gazing at me
When a bright door in, my eyes do see.

Anger Rays

As wine, some words are so old
And their seekers are few,
When abundant, is the fake gold
As wine troubled and new.
But beware, the waves are rough
And your ships built of pines,
Will suffer when cedar wood tough
Is piled on shore in lines.

Biased Judgment (Haiku)

Almonds mock olives

Under sun, before almonds

Return back to sleep.

Sonnet 06

How with such abundant rivers you speak
And murmuring your uttered words do sound,
Within your hair, countless falls slide and seek
Upon your shoulders, tinted bloom be found.
How your eyes a limitless space convey
Where countless stars all the heed they steal,
Tell me then how, upon your cheeks, buds stay
All year long in mid spring lively appeal.
How can your fresh lips, in all ripe fruits glow
And pour sweetness across your mild chin
To your neck, that softly does glide and flow
Down to where I write oft, with my own skin.
Shall I have you, as much as I desire?
Or continent shall I be, nigh your fire?

The Dawn's Break

I just turned a full rusty page
And almost tore it apart
My fingers raced with full rage
Eager for a new start
Now a page blank and white
Hungry and virgin still
Summoning ink day and night
That its emptiness will kill.

Human Theatre (Haiku)

We don't see in nature,
Some tigers eat mice, some deer,
Tigers are equal.

Sonnet 07

The deck is clean and unusually dry
The sails are full battling the anchor
Wives have shed tears, with a deep cry
For their men on the ship seek and hanker
After the vast limitless wealthy blue
That gives and steals and kills and heals.
The mast is ready, stern, and new
And the eager sails it holds and feels
They say that sailors' first tears after birth
Are seen by the restless foamy waves
And ever since, the sea fills with mirth
The seafarers' longings until their graves
Hurry! Pull the anchor now, help me fast
Ere my heart runs back to my land of past

A Longing

With a big basket, I got out one day,
To get oranges from the field.
But an apple captured me on the way,
It had memories within its red,
A hundred stories concealed.
I stopped and thought,
And gazed and brought,
That single apple, as all my yield!

Human School (Haiku)

Eagles teach their youngs,
How to hunt and rule the skies,
Rabbits, how to flee.

Sonnet 08

Backwards, at the cradle a look I cast,
At the unreachable old heedless years,
No memory of mine can touch that past,
When unaware, I gave smiles and tears.
Then I look at "now", undoubtedly clean,
My memory is at rest, for my eye
Depicts my present, so sharply seen
If it's surely mine, I can hold it. Can't I?
Then again, I look, again, but this time
I know not, how many years to there,
At my silent grave, I send my rhyme
No smiles, no tears, I'll give unaware.
How can I call mine, those dear flowing times?
Into their sacred stream, I lay down my rhymes.

Wise Years

(Written in Terza Rima)

A lesson I learned o'er the years
Through my mind numb and thick
Of how I gave my smiles and tears,
At times when I was really sick
I wondered why injustice ruled,
And wished time to pass quick.
Only when I got my health tuned
And regained my force, I thought
Not of my illness past wound
But justice in my words I sought,
And wished time to slowly pass
And beauty I sang and taught.

Self-hate (Haiku)

Once a rose hated
Its very thorns, for they harmed
Its only lover.

Sonnet 09

In Autumn, you felt the glooming falling days,
Your colours dimmed and scarily you sought
What could soothe your darkening pale rays
And saw me, so to my place you brought
Your dreams and hopes, your waves and slopes.
In Winter, you beat with my warm beats,
To my square you bind firmly with thick ropes
Your thin hollow self and through my sheets.
Then thicker you grew in Spring's warm ground
Coloured, you loosened yourself from me
As you espied life was yielding around,
And slowly you did slide in Summer and flee.
Autumn's here, glooming days reign once more,
I see your thin hollow wave, nighing my shore.

True Love

If I lit in my place of some wood a fire
And the flies of dark came
If my bright flames went higher and higher
Gathering around it the lame
What would all of them hide and fold
What would the reason be?
Would it be of the love they bear and hold
For warmth, for light, or for me?

A Smile (Haiku)

When she smiled, I saw
Blooms of daisies and lilies
Roses and orchids.

Sonnet 10

A snow, a mist, maybe a ghost, a cloud,
On Lebanon's secluded high peaks
As praying souls, from the frosty ground
Up to the near sky, a hazy fog leaks.
I exhale a warmth, a strain I do shed,
An icy breeze with cedar wood scent
Through my nostrils to my deep heart is led,
And my sight falls upon the mighty age bent.
An upwards hand with spiky, dark green
Merrily burdened with the purest white
That glows with a chilling, eye-blazing sheen.
At the Cedars of God, my tenth I write.
Timeless are the words of sonnets they say,
Thus, if I write them, they timelessly stay.

Chained

While I was having a walk
With none beside me to talk
Burdened with society's laws
Thoughtful about all my flaws.
Disturbed by all the conflicts I wore
And the lack of peace, I saw on shore
A fisherman with clothes torn
As life had left him forlorn.
I neared to behold his tanned face
Where a serene smile took place
I envied the tranquillity he wore
As if he owned the whole shore.
He looked at me, "How are you, son?"
In silence and in words, he won!

"I'm fine," I said and then I asked
About the secret which his smile masked.
His eyes were drawn to the open sea
Then they looked and smiled at me
"As free as the open blue, you see
I lived, and if I die, I'll die free."

Martyrs (Haiku)

The breaths of killed trees,
Blow alive within the fifes,
In killers' keen hands.

Sonnet 11

Into a dense forest I once passed by
Shy sun rays barely nuzzled the loam
I turned my head up, and looked high
Then, I beheld into a big tree's dome
A captivating suspended deep blue
An orchid that my eyes had never seen
That mid-forest art with a marine hue
Captured my heart and mind by its sheen
Couldn't walk on save after I climbed up
And plucked the blossom with my hand
With outstretched roots I winded it up
And from that forest, I took it to my land.
Do all the beloved ones if moved away
From their land, as that orchid, pass away?

The Two Faces (Haiku)

Moderation is,
Pleasure's friendliest ally,
And its deadly foe.

Sonnet 12

Waves of dusty past, crushing against my shore
With foam half white, haphazardly widespread
And thunderous squashing of half-heard yore
That write on my sand some words barely read.
Algae of half-forgotten, dismantled trust
Cling every now and then to my coastal rocks.
A frothy mass of love, hate, fear and lust
Messing with the speed of hands in my clocks.
This stormy sea that rarely boils and smashes
My sand and rocks, besides my doors and locks
Summons old, renewed memories and flashes,
And brings turbulent waters in my calm docks.
So great, my mountains I behold and see,
When my back I turn, to my turbulent sea.

A Lamenting Soul

One day, my door was opened wide
And a pilgrim stood there
I invited him by my side
And offered him a chair.
"For sure," I said, "you roam a lot
Across the mist and tide
You seek the truth, to heal the rot
What's your quest by my side?"
"Not a truth seeker, not to heal
I roam only to hide,"
Thus, he did say and cry and kneel
And weep long, by my side.

Sonnet 13

A sunny day, in chilling, twisted mind
Bears a breath of summer, so far and lost
As if winter has forgotten to wind
Its clock and now losing its very frost
I rove while my senses travel to you
What would you do, in such a sudden break
From dim streets, and clouds with dismal hue
What would you say, if you did not forsake
The air that adored you like my heart did?
If you sailed not, into the foggy sea
Where foul death behind comely words hid
Oh, how I wish that you can now feel me
'Tis good, a strong wind brings clouds o'er my head
And all those thoughts, out of my mind are led.

Time (Haiku)

If we're sad, you're slow

We laugh you haste, 'ere you go

As warm ice you thaw.

Sonnet 14

I had a feeling while I was asleep,
I felt it, a benediction in my dream!
It went across my spine to my heart deep
As if my soul had caught a heavenly beam.
As warmth in mid-winter, it came to me,
As prayer to a dreary and sick soul,
As rain to a parched land, as a shady tree
To a sun-bruised walker who lost control.
I sensed, I knew, I heard, I felt your pace
Nearing and entering softly my room
I opened then, my eyes to your smiley face
And woke up to your ever yielding bloom.
Those days, my awakening was better with you.
Now I love to sleep, to dream and see you through.

The Breeze that Loved Me

You came to me in the yestermorn
A gentle movement, a breeze
You knew then that a bond was born
And time went to freeze.
Then at noon, you grew a wind
And shook the bond you built
You looked at me as an odd fiend
It thundered awe and fear and guilt.
At yestereve, you broke the bond
A raging storm, you sang free
Tell me now; why are you calm and fond?
This morning, a breeze you come to me?!

Sonnet 15

They grow, they change, and within our own eyes
We watch their smiles, we attend their tears
Then, as an autumn leaf before it dies
They give their green to their yellowing years.
What rack, what hurt, what agony, what pain
Can we carry with them, to soothe their woe?
Though we much want, our wishes are in vain,
For each has a time and a way to go.
The will of a human is great indeed
The way a grain of sand is great as well,
When humans run after a shiny need
A sandstorm blows unseen, and rings their bell
Aside a river, when I sit and gaze,
With passing waters, I see passing days.

Justice (Haiku)

The strongest is slow,
The fastest is weak. As tides,
Either high, or low.

Sonnet 16

I met the memory of you today,
It was beautiful, as you used to be
We talked and laughed and walked the same way,
We were just as you and I used to be.
The trees saw us and they were fondly glad,
The roads recognised our pace once again,
As if the united heartbeats we had
Were back, ravishing and vernal and sane.
Words were old, yet we played them well and new,
As fresh as the buds of this early spring
In a morning that's still covered with dew,
Sparkling like your eyes and the joy they bring.
Said I missed you, it said you missed me too
Wasn't sure, was it your memory, or you.

Sonnet 17

Darkness does not subsist, as does light,
For the two, when combined, can't coexist,
Need I sit and wonder, and then I write
Of a place, far and near and ever lit.
To a never-empty well, my thoughts sink
Hastily, as if burdened with parched thirst,
Which leaves me in heedful silence to think
About what is moving my soul at first.
If thirst is dark and water's truly bright,
The deep well shines then, with a gorgeous sheen,
And the sunny place above, a black night
That a beam of blest light has never seen.
O Mighty, I sensed thy water, thy good,
When neath sun, nigh a well, thirsty I stood.

A Secret

Thus, it fell
Under a spell
I loved you
But couldn't tell

Deep inside
A fond high tide
Of burning flames
Dwells and hides

Sonnet 18

At a desk I sought my aim blest and curst,
I found it not, but what I got right there
Was a blazing shot that my dormant thirst
Did shake and wake and spread into the air.
At that desk I sat, then to me she came,
As thirsty as the desert sand, she neared
And neared some more, till we lost our first aim,
I had her water and she had mine cleared.
A talk, a touch, a walk, a gaze, a kiss,
Then into the sheets of a bright warm nest
We drank from each other's well with hot bliss,
Quenching a parched lust that burned in the chest.
Hunger decays where plenty of food dwells,
As thirst when thrown into a bed of wells.

A Nature's Court

With an abundance of flowers
White as morning snow,
An almond tree, neath sun showers
Smiled and with pride did glow
It looked at a near olive tree
And despised its dark green
That lacked the vernal dress and glee
As a gloomy sad scene.
Winter came with its colour thieves,
The naked almond glanced
And envied the dense olive leaves
That, with winter winds danced.

Sonnet 19

Across the sacred heath I step and walk,
Shrubs of words bind my aimless soul, a whole
I breathe in silence, yet my breaths talk
To Thy Holy Ears that know well my goal.
From afar, I behold a neat, bright tree
That to my senses talks with great reasons,
I see it nearing, as if sailing free
As if it knows no roots, and no seasons.
I welcome those fruits of delicious look
Which locks my eyes, towards that deep red
And haunts my sweet desires, as a hook
That no human can escape its firm thread.
Forgive me if by body or by thought,
Away from Thy Face, my pleasure I sought.

Inner Pain (Haiku)

Bleeding wounds and scars
Of a sick heart, can be veiled
With a woman's smile.

Sonnet 20

I hear the sound of weeping with the wind
Blowing into your naked limbs so still,
As if a raging soul of a killed fiend
Is avenging the love of its dear kill.
I sense death inhabiting your thick trunk
As you hold up leafless week after week,
As if life has passed you heedlessly drunk
And left you bare and raw and cold and weak.
Not a shelter for dank birds you can be,
Nor a cloak for a passer-by to rest,
Nor a sight that the eye delights to see,
Not even a place for an empty nest!
A warm breeze my cold cheeks pleasantly feel,
O Might! Your branches are sprouting for real.

Sonnet 21

In gloomy days, I go out to the shores
Where the waves pull to them my suffering,
Then my heart with the soaring seagulls soars
Accepting the sky and its offering.
The foamy white is to my weary eyes
What moonlight is to a blackish night,
And the mist that aimlessly roams and flies
Rests on my face after a dreary fight.
I close my eyes and feel the colder mist
That to my depth sends a kind, soothing touch,
All at once, my pain ceases to exist,
So, I smile without asking further much
This gloomy day, I went out to the sea
And a dead seagull fell in front of me.

A Show

They envy my garment of red
That glitters when a light thread,
Without a touch passes near
As if to my skin is dear.
And a reddish hue I spread.
They envy my lines when they fight
Corruption in its shameless night,
The beauty of some rhyming words,
That one day, will slash as swords.
And a just flame will ignite.
Oh, my ink, of burden you flow
With a heavy breath you blow to glow,
Oh, my skin of fervid bleed,
Your red is all what most will read.
Just another passing show.

Sonnet 22

I gaze at death and then I gaze at you,
With closed eyes I sink to my own self, deep,
I find a nightingale that the thick dew
Has soaked its wings and sent them into sleep.
I find a nightingale whose known loud voice
Is now burdened with doubt and barely heard,
Each time it wants by a song to rejoice
An old vow comes across and chokes the bird.
As if past that lives still in form of blame,
And a dew of a never-ending dawn,
They both reside to keep my creature tame
In a wet cage at the end of life's lawn.
What an instant! In which I break the cage,
And shatter its bars with tremendous rage.

Sonnet 23

Down to a grave that would never be seen,
To that dark silence with faith, I put you,
And left you there, my one and only bean,
Where no sun, no wind, no sight and no hue.
Down to a pit where stillness and demise
Sing a lullaby of slumber to earth,
So that the abyssal exhausted eyes
Know no day, no night, no sadness, no mirth.
As iron in the blazing fire heat,
As caterpillars in their muted sleep,
The life-giving sun you shall seek and meet
When you send your roots into the dark deep.
Thus, when my limbs grow limp, and my thoughts die,
As a bean with faith shall I rest and lie.

A Micro Poem

Like a candle,
She shone on me,
Then disappeared.

Sonnet 24

Vernal, lively flowers with colours high,
Envied the hated dull thorns on thy head,
The earth and the sky, as temples did cry,
And with the drops of thy clear blood, they bled.
Terror and fear, reigned with horror and dread,
Amidst the shaitans of the rancid deep,
As they distinguished thee among the dead,
And in their canyons of hell did weep.
Thy sun shineth upon the obscure needs,
Thy wisdom shaketh the mind of the wit,
Thy peace, purifieth hearts from vile deeds,
Heavens are from thy splendor ever lit.
Through a drop of dew, the vast sky I see,
It thrills my thoughts, and my thoughts drift to thee.

Desires

Once I loved a root
And that root loved me
It kept sucking me
It took all my goods
Till I was left nearly empty
Then I loved a branch
And that branch loved me
It kept giving me goods
Fruits and leaves
till I left
With painful uselessness.
It was only when
I loved a whole vine
And that vine loved me
That I was satisfied
And put into peace.

Relativity and Beauty

Relativity cannot affect beauty,
It rather touches the capacity
Of satisfying the diverse needs.

Sonnet 25

How I long for a cool breeze when I sit
In summer's heat and wet air in my cot,
Oh, how I miss those cold days barely lit
When beneath the full bright sun, I walk hot.
But when those cold days are finally here
And the winds of deadly ice my cot meet,
I miss that sun, and wish those rays are near
I wish to walk under the yellow heat.
In times of lengthy silence, I do seek
Some talk, some noise, some footsteps and some sound
Then, through a chaotic and noisy week
How I miss deep silence being around.
But maiden, heed that you're never the case
Nigh or far, I much admire your face.

The Caterpillar that Never Flew

Once, a thought came to my mind
It was spring blooming around,
That thought did flourish and find
As a seed, its way out of ground.

Then, to my hands and eyes
As vernal colours it shone,
Straight out of its disguise
A full poem at early dawn.

Seasons passed, as rivers did flow
Hastening towards the sea,
Flowers did change and did grow
Into dead ghosts inside of me.

Then, a thought appeared again
It was winter glooming around,
Clouds where heavy and the rain
Was rhyming the dark ground.

So, to my mind that thought came
But not to my hands and eyes,
It grew fragile, it grew lame
For no sun was in the skies.

No poem nor any work showed there
And that thought poisoned me,
That's true, they say, and that's fair.
A caterpillar is meant to roam the air.
Otherwise, pestilent would be.

Sonnet 26

I lost your face when you left for too long
Between the ancient thoughts of my childhood,
And still, when to my ears sings an old song
Your memory strikes from a time so good.
I lost your voice when you forever slept
Between the dark pillows of running time,
Still, it echoes as if your words have kept
Their place within my never-ending rhyme.
As perfect as the ever-moving earth,
As restless as the ever-crushing waves,
A flame is hitting with sorrow and mirth,
So, I shall feed the empty white that craves.
I lost your face, I lost your voice, indeed,
But here I am, holding them, as a seed.

Sonnet 27

Between the gorgeous daisies I do walk
Fully aware not to step over them,
To the petals of pure white I do talk
When I approach a flower by the stem.
I recall to my colour-sensing mind
This painted moving field few months ago,
Back then if I searched, I could never find
A green, a red, a white, or a yellow.
They say that in the winter's gloomy womb
Lives the coming spring, unseen and timid,
And what seems to be a blackish brown tomb
Holds beneath the lively hues so vivid.
At the tomb of a beloved, I stand,
I hold a daisy, and my heart in hand.

Sonnet 28

An empty wide street I look down to see
Around each corner a ghostly presence,
Dusty pathways look back and gaze at me
And in my hollow soul, search for pleasance.
Echoes of distant laughter and long talks
Tease with craving longings my silent ear,
Along with the footsteps of late-night walks
That are now chained by disabling fear.
I wonder how with each breeze I can smell
Your distinctive scent that I much long for,
And how your shades as if sent by a spell
Haunt my numb eyes to miss you even more.
This street is empty, save of very few,
And my heart is full, with the trace of you.

Sonnet 29

A seedless oaken tree, when buried whole
Beneath the life-giving forest rich soil,
Decays, and to its green leaves, death will crawl
With no speediness, no sound, no turmoil.
But what we must all attentively heed,
Is that when below the wealthy fine ground
Instead of the oak tree, an acorn seed
Is put and into the dark earth is bound,
Life will greet it, and down to the black deep
As well as up to the bright sun and sky,
That acorn with roots firm and branches steep
Will sprout and grow astonishingly high.
How many people we live with and know,
are acorns, and others like oak trees grow?

The Shades of Beauty

At noon I took
A philosophy book,
And went in need
For a long read.
I found a rock
Then set my clock

Aside it rose
A wine-red rose
Its shade was clear
It was a sphere
At its base it sat
On the earth flat.

Then, after soon
Came afternoon
I read and read
And the rose red
Near it stood
Gorgeously good.

Its shade was clear
But not a sphere!
It changed and took
The rose's look
Longer did lay
A bit away.

I read and read
In Plato's thread
And the bright sun
Had already begun
Towards the sea
To run and flee.

And the rose stood
Unchangeably good
But oh! Its shade
Began to fade
Longer it grew
On darkening hue.

I closed my book
My time I took
The sun was gone
After it shone
And that rose stood
Always good.

But no shade was there
No sun in the air
I went home and thought
About what I brought
In my thinking brain
What could remain.

Relativity cannot affect Beauty (the rose),
It rather touches the capacity of satisfying
The diverse needs and desires (the shades).

Sonnet 30

On high, steep rocks within the winds forlorn,
Greeted by sun, guarded by angel eyes,
In a golden nest my first breath was born,
I saw naught but felt the vast open skies.
I sensed the warm rays on my bare weak skin,
Yet when they were much, I sensed a cool shade,
As if my body which was faint and thin
Had no reason to be tense or afraid.
When my eyes opened, I saw by my side
Love and fondness and strength and wise caring,
They fed me till I was feathered and wide
But oh! they were slain when I was staring.
I am no longer small, no longer weak,
I'll ride winds, with death on my claws and beak.

About the Author

Ziad is a Lebanese poet and artist, interested in the pursuit of beauty and a higher self. English is his third language, yet the most loved one when it comes to literary works.

After studying English Literature and Painting, mostly influenced by Vincent Van Gogh, Gibran Kahlil Gibran, William Blake and other romantics, he started his own journey of writing and painting.

Beholding a poet, as a nightingale, with a vastly misunderstood language, our author is known as the "Lebanese Nightingale" started a journey of words and colours.

INKFEATHERS PUBLISHING

India's Most Author Friendly Publishing House

Stay updated about the latest books, anthologies, events, exclusive offers, contests, product giveaways and other things that we do to support authors.

Inkfeathers Publishing

@InkfeathersPublishing

@_Inkfeathers

@Inkfeathers

Inkfeathers.com

We'd love to connect with you!